What to doodle?

AT SCHOOL

John Kurtz

DOVER PUBLICATIONS, INC.
Mineola, New York

NOTE

Here are some of the challenges that you'll find in this fun-filled book: Draw a school basketball team, create art in the playground, and add a map of Africa to a chalkboard. Come up with your own ideas for finishing the pictures—then color your drawings!

Bibliographical Note

What to Doodle? At School, first published by Dover Publications, Inc., in 2013, is a republication of a selection of material from the previously published work *What to Doodle? My World!* (Dover Publications, Inc., 2013) in a different form.

International Standard Book Number

ISBN-13: 978-0-486-49229-2
ISBN-10: 0-486-49229-X

Manufactured in the United States by Courier Corporation
49229X03   2014
www.doverpublications.com

Megan is 8 years old today.
Draw cupcakes to share at school.

Can you help Al write on the chalkboard?

Draw the fish they see in the tank on a school trip to the aquarium.

Draw what is in the backpack on the desk.

Draw the rest of the school basketball team.

Draw the bells she is ringing at the school play.

Draw the big bug that Jerry brought
to show and tell.

7

What have they built with all the blocks?

Draw books in the classroom bookcase.

Fran loves butterflies. Draw the butterflies
she brought to school!

What instrument is Bill playing? Draw it!

Draw the chalk art on the school playground.

Draw the classroom plant that Sonia has watered.

Monica is studying clouds in science class.
Draw clouds in the sky!

Draw a pattern on the cloth on the wall.

Draw big buttons on the cloth.

Jamie has brought his castle project to class.
Show it!

Help Tim finish drawing the bear on the board.

Finish drawing the giraffe.

Draw a penguin from the South Pole.

Draw the planet Saturn on the board.

Draw his best friend from school.

Draw her best friend from school.

Draw a map of Africa on the board.

Draw the school that Zach will attend.

Draw the big dinosaur at the museum.

Mark and Linda have glued something
together. Draw it!

Sam has brought his grandmother
to school. Draw her.

Sandie has brought her grandfather
to school. Draw him.

Draw the hamster in the classroom.

Draw a long jump rope!

What kind of ball is he kicking? Draw it.

What does Jason see out the window?

What is the school lunch for today?

What does Julian see in the microscope? Draw it!

Draw the instrument Joe is playing.

Finish the paper chain!

What pet has Susan brought to school? Draw it.

What is Emily petting on the school trip
to the petting zoo?

Draw the vase that Selena is making
in pottery class.

What is Lewis pushing down the hallway at school?

Draw the fun game they are playing.

Draw a picture of what Craig is reading.

Draw the items that you recycle the most.

Touchdown! Draw the football players.

Draw the flag on the flagpole.

Draw North and South America on the globe.

Draw some more classmates to
act in the play with Alex.

Draw what the friends are playing catch with.

Draw what Gina is heating up in science class.

What has Evan made with paper and scissors?

Draw the sculpture that Carlos had made.

Kenny is the shortest boy in class.
Draw his friend Quinn, the tallest.

Roy has a surprise for show and tell. Draw it!

Andy has brought his stamp collection to school.
Draw his favorite stamp.

Paula wants to be a doctor someday.
Draw a skeleton she can study.

Draw the rest of the swingset and a
friend to swing with.

What did the teacher write for math homework?

Draw the musical notes coming from the trumpet.

Draw lots of smoke from the volcano!

Time to take the bus home! Draw it!

What does Greg want to be when he grows up?